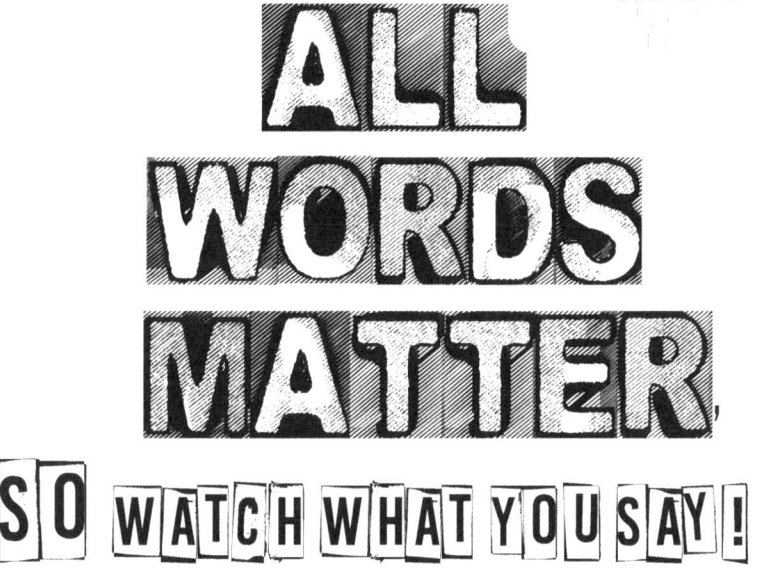

ALL WORDS MATTER, SO WATCH WHAT YOU SAY!

Pastor Helen R. Kinloch

www.TrueVinePublishing.org

All Words Matter, So...Watch What You Say...
Helen R. Kinloch

Published by:
True Vine Publishing Co. LLC
810 Dominican Dr. Ste. 103
Nashville, TN 37228
www.TrueVinePublishing.org

Unless otherwise noted, all scriptures taken from the Holy Bible, King James Version.

ISBN: 978-1-956469-46-2 Paperback
ISBN: 978-1-956469-47-9 eBook

Printed in the United States of America—First Printing

DEDICATION

First, all honor and praise go to my Lord and Savior, Jesus Christ, for without Him this book would not exist. I dedicate this book to my husband, Flash Kinloch, Sr.—my soul mate chosen by God to assist me in the work of ministry. Thank you for your patience and understanding as I pursue another chapter of my life.

TABLE OF CONTENTS

ACKNOWLEDGMENTS

Thank you to my six children, who continuously help me to evolve as a person. I especially want to acknowledge my daughter, Gabrielle, for tirelessly working with me to complete edits. Also, to Keturah Ruth who did the original transcribing of the sermons that created this book. Thank you for navigating through pages of notes.

To my first-born, Flash Jr. Your encouraging words, continual support, and motivation mean more to me than you'll ever know.

Special thanks to a great team: Sharon for finding and coordinating with the publisher, Doris for ordering the wristbands for the project, Kedyky for administrative support, and Katrina for always supporting me and giving great ideas.

Last, but certainly not least, thank you to God's Way Church Family for all your love and support. Seeing your lives transformed through

God's word continues to inspire me every day.

PREFACE

At the end of February 2022, after I completed a series of teachings on sonship, I prayed and sought the Father for what I would be ministering to His people next. He revealed to me that He wanted His people to really grasp the truth that what they say matters because of who they are—sons and daughters of God. As I started preparing the messages for the series, the Holy Spirit spoke to me about the importance of the teachings. Although I had given a similar message in the past, I felt that this time it was different.

The Lord revealed that many believers are committing spiritual suicide. He revealed to me that His children are destroying their families, losing jobs and businesses, battling sicknesses and diseases, and some are even dying prematurely because of the words they speak. They are unaware of the truth that their words are creating the

9

lives they are living. They were being destroyed because of lack of knowledge (Hosea 4:6). He wanted me to tell them that because they are children of the Creator (God), as believers, what they say matters. Therefore, it is imperative that they watch what they are releasing out of their mouths.

After I shared this series with the congregation and others, I quickly understood why this time was different than before. So many people shared with me how it never occurred to them they were essentially speaking against their own lives and ultimately hindering their progress. As a result of the series and the daily reminder bracelets they were given, their lives were being transformed. Therefore, it is my prayer that you will use these same Biblical principles and strategies, given in the simplest form throughout this book, to transform your own life in extraordinary ways.

INTRODUCTION

This book is small in size. However, the contents, if followed, will have the biggest impact on your life. It will literally transform the way you speak, think, and view the world around you. If you believe these instructions, they will work for you. The foundation on which this book stands is based on the principles found in the first book of the Bible: Genesis 1, in addition to Proverbs 18:21 and Proverbs 13:3. In these books of the Bible, you will find strategies, revelation, and wisdom that are often overlooked but critical to creating the life you desire.

Note that the Bible says in Deuteronomy 29:29, "The secret things belong to the LORD our God, but the things that are revealed belong to us and to our children forever, that we may do all the words of this law." Therefore, in this book, you will find God-given strategies that will help you in every area of your life. These strategies are God-inspired and based upon His written word. They have the power to change your health, business, finances, relationships, and most of all your life.

At the end of this book, you will find real testimonies of people young and old, who have used these principles to produce miraculous results in their lives. In addition, you will be given information on how you can receive your own wristband that has the phrase, "Watch What You Say" on it as well as the scripture Proverbs 18:21, *(Death and life are in the power of the tongue, and they who indulge in it shall eat the fruit of it [for death or life])* to serve as a daily reminder that your words matter. Therefore, *Watch What You Say!*

BEGIN BY BELIEVING

Before you can receive or manifest that which you desire using the power of your words, you must begin by believing. In other words, if you want the strategies and principles in this book to work in your life, you must believe and have faith in God's word. God is the creator of the universe, and He has given His children the same spirit of faith according to II Corinthians 4:13.

A benefit of having the same spirit of faith as God is that you have the ability to create your own world as He did in Genesis 1. Ephesians 5:1 states, you should be an imitator of God as His dear child, for He called the things that be not as though they were (Romans 4:17). In the midst of darkness and voidness, God said, "Let there be" and it was (Genesis 1:3). Therefore, you must be confident in whose you are and who you are whenever you release faith-filled words out of your mouth. Like the Creator, your words are never empty. If you have faith and believe in your God-given ability to create, you can have whatever it is that you say. Before a word leaves your mouth, remember that you must believe to receive.

"Truly I tell you, if anyone says to this mountain, 'Go, throw yourself into the sea,' and does not doubt in their heart but believes that what they say will happen, it will be done for them," Mark 11:23.

Believe that your words have the power to create!

BELIEF JOURNAL

What do you believe?

TAKE INVENTORY - MONITOR YOUR WORDS

First things first. If you want this book to work in your life, you must commit to the work. While it may not be easy from the onset, it is not complicated. This book will help simplify things for you. As you progress through each of the strategies, you will begin to understand how they work together to produce your desired results.

Therefore, whenever you truly want to account for certain things in your life, both tangible and intangible, taking inventory is a good place to start. In doing this, you can precisely see the relationship between what you say and what you ultimately see manifested in your life. So, when it comes to words that you speak or have spoken, it is important that the first thing you do is take inventory of some of the things that you have said and what you are saying daily — both positive and negative, and then monitor what you say.

Most people would probably agree that this is not an easy task. In fact, it requires discipline and honesty to be effective. It does not matter how you choose to monitor your speech; however, the most important thing is that you are aware of what you are saying about whatever areas of your life you have chosen to focus on. Some people may choose to recall things spoken in the past while others will simply write out words being spoken in the present. Regardless of the method, your goal for the next few days is to take inventory of the words that you are speaking.

Monitor your words.

WORDS JOURNAL

Strategy: Monitor your words and account for what you are speaking, positive or negative. Use the following journal pages to record your words over the next 3 days.

_____

_____

_____

_____

_____

_____

_____

_____

_____

_____

_____

_____

_____

_____

_____

_____

Day 1:

Day 2:

Day 3:

WHAT ARE YOU DECLARING?

Have you ever thought of the fact that what you see around you (your life) is a direct result of some of the things that you have spoken? As spiritual beings, you must be mindful of the things you are declaring over your life each day, whether it is intentional or not. If most people were honest with themselves, they would admit that most of the time, they are reckless with their words and often speak from an emotional or reactionary state of mind. Not only this, but they are neither consistent, persistent, or focused when it comes to things that they want to be manifested in their lives.

One moment, they are speaking and declaring positive affirmations over their lives, and the next, they are cursing everything in their path. What then is the outcome? More than likely, it is not the desired outcome. As a result, they become depressed and impatient, not realizing that their words are truly powerful enough to produce and manifest things in the natural world.

Think about this: One day, you begin declaring positive words about a particular area of your life, and the next day something unexpected happens in that area that causes you to speak negatively. The last thing you declared or spoke into the atmosphere, which was negative, cancels out the positive. It does not go away. It will remain the prevailing outcome in that area of your life.

Every day you must be intentional to consistently declare positive things if you want to see them come to fruition. How do you speak positive things consistently? You make it a habit. It is said that anything done consistently for 21 days, can become a habit. When positive consistent declaration becomes a habit, it can produce great things in your life!

Make positive, consistent declarations a daily habit.

POSITIVE DECLARATIONS JOURNAL

Write out a list of positive declarations to speak over your life, daily.

SELF-SABOTAGE

It is so unfortunate that many people are not aware of the truth that their words have power. Your words have the power to create, destroy, or maintain anything you purpose in your heart. The Bible states in Proverbs 12:18 that quick thoughtless words are like a sword. It will kill you, but if you are wise with your words, it will bring healing. With this in mind, there is a very familiar scientific experiment that studied the effects of speaking positive words versus negative words to a plant.

In this study, the plant that received positive or encouraging words spoken daily over it thrived, while the plant that received negative or discouraging words died. Why did this happen? This happened because God, the Creator, has given man the power and unique ability to use words to bring about whatever he desires to see manifested.

Therefore, it is imperative that you do not hinder your progress with your own negative words. Do not sabotage your future, especially because of your emotions.

As a powerful speaking being, you must always be conscious of your emotional state to avoid self-sabotage. Often when people experience difficulties and the pressures of life, they speak words out of their mouths through frustration and anger. For example, someone may say, "It seems like I am always sick," or "As soon as I get money, it is gone." While these words may be a figure of speech or what they are accustomed to saying, once it is released out of the mouth and into the atmosphere, they will receive the results of what they have spoken.

Therefore, they will always be sick and never be able to keep money. Psalm 141:3 reads, "Set a guard over my mouth, Lord, keep watch over the door of my lips." This scripture emphasizes the importance of watching what you say, regardless of your emotional state. As a result, if you are believing, praying, or asking God to do something in your life and it seems that it is not happening, check your emotions at the door of your lips. It may be the one thing that is hindering your blessing.

Be aware of your emotions.

EMOTIONS JOURNAL

Which Emotions / Emotional Triggers should you be aware of this week?

_____

_____

_____

_____

_____

_____

_____

_____

_____

_____

_____

_____

_____

_____

_____

_____

_____

_____

WHAT YOU SAY MATTERS

"Sticks and stones may break your bones, but words **CAN AND WILL HURT YOU!"**

Whether you believe it or not, what you say matters to the life you desire to live. The Bible states in John 1:1, *"In the beginning was the word and the word was with God, and the word was God."* Your Creator created this universe by the power of His words. Therefore, it is evident that the blueprint for creating the world you desire is through the power of words.

Every word that you speak produces some result in your life. In the book of James 1:19 it states, "Be quick to listen, slow to speak, and slow to become angry." Why should you be slow to speak? It is because, "By your words, you are justified or condemned" (Matthew 12:37).

Therefore, you must always choose your words wisely. Words can encourage, tear down, kill, hurt, build up, destroy, and ultimately change lives positively or negatively. As a believer created in God's image and likeness, you have the same power to speak as He spoke and the world around you must produce that which was spoken.

However, most people are not conscious of the fact that both positive and negative words equally produce results. Life and death are in the power of the tongue (Proverbs 18:21). This means EVERYTHING you speak, whether good or bad, has the power to produce whatever was spoken. Words are always at work. The emotional circumstances surrounding the words you speak do not prevent negative words from having an impact on your reality. It does not matter if you are angry, happy, sad, or disappointed. Once words are released from your mouth they will produce after their kind. With the same mouth, you can build or kill your plans, goals, and dreams.

The great, wise, and noble King Solomon

stated in Proverbs 13:3, "He that keeps (watch over, guard, maintain, refrain) his mouth, keeps his life, but he that opens wide his lips shall have destruction." When you guard what you say, it can protect, preserve, and save your life. However, to the contrary, when you open your mouth recklessly (without thinking) it will bring destruction. Remember, "Be careful little mouth what you say."

Guard your mouth!

JOURNAL

Replacing Negative with Positive. Write down some of the reckless negative statements you make on the left row, and a positive alternative you can use instead on the right.

Negative	Positive Alternative
_____	_____
_____	_____
_____	_____
_____	_____
_____	_____
_____	_____
_____	_____
_____	_____
_____	_____
_____	_____
_____	_____
_____	_____
_____	_____
_____	_____
_____	_____
_____	_____

WATCH WHAT YOU SAY

As a believer, you have the ability to go a step further when it comes to watching what you say. In fact, this strategy will help you to truly put your belief and faith into action. In the previous strategies, you have learned that to watch what you say, means to put a guard over your mouth so you speak positive, faithful words. It also means to be mindful of the words you are speaking about a situation or any area of your life.

However, it is equally important that you also think of this concept (watch what you say) from another perspective. The Bible says in Jeremiah 1:12, "The Lord said to me…for I am watching to see that my word is fulfilled." This scripture reveals that the Lord actively watches over His words to perform it.

Are you watching over the words that you have spoken? Are you looking every day with expectation? This strategy is twofold. When you watch what you say (guard your mouth so that you speak positively), you must also watch (look with expectations for your words to produce) what you say. Watching is an act of faith. It is active and on-going. Do not forget this important strategy.

Watch (look with expectation for your words to produce.)

EXPECTATION JOURNAL

What do your words look like? List your expected outcomes based on what you have been declaring each day.

_____

_____

_____

_____

_____

_____

_____

_____

_____

_____

_____

_____

_____

_____

_____

_____

21 DAYS OF FASTING FROM NEGATIVE WORDS

When you hear the word "fasting," one, more than likely, assumes that it pertains to food. This kind of fast normally involves abstaining from specific kinds of food or completely removing all food from your diet for a period of time. There are countless studies and even examples throughout the Bible that have shown the benefits of fasting in this form. However, fasting in combination with food is not the only type of fasting that can be beneficial for you.

Now that you understand the power your words possess and the strategies that will bring about the life you desire, it is time to put your belief and faith into action. For the next 21 days, you will fast from negative unproductive words. During this time, you should refrain from reacting negatively to what you see, hear, or feel but instead respond positively with what you want that situation to be.

Remember to be mindful of your emotions as it can cause you to respond erratically, without consideration of the words you are releasing. This is the time for you to be intentional and careful with your words. Therefore, remember to keep in mind what you read in the previous section "Watch What You Say." Every word you release is alive and active. It will produce! Therefore, choose your words wisely.

*During your fast, use the bracelet to help you remember to watch what you say. Invite family and friends to join you.

Fast from negative words.

Use the space below to note any specific areas of struggle. For example, note if you have difficulty watching what you say when you experience certain emotions.

_____

_____

_____

_____

_____

_____

_____

_____

_____

_____

_____

_____

_____

_____

_____

DIVINE STRATEGIES TO CREATE YOUR WORLD

If you want to begin creating the life and world that you desire, look no further than the example given to mankind by God—the creator of the universe. While there are many books published about how to create your own world, there is one book that is often overlooked, although it is easily accessible to most of the world. From the beginning of creation, the Bible shows in Genesis 1, that God had a divine strategy in motion as He created the universe from a state of voidness. For seven days, He said **what He wanted, and He saw the manifestation of those things**.

Not only was God specific with His words, but each day, He specifically focused on a particular area. On the first day, He created light; the second day, firmament which is Heaven; on the third day, dry land, plants, etc.; on the fourth day, the sun, moon, and stars; on the fifth day, fish, and fowls; on the sixth day, animals and man; and on the seventh day, He rested. Everything created had a set day. God was specific and He spoke what He wanted to come into existence.

Genesis does not reveal a God who was confused about what He wanted. It also does not tell of a God who is trying to accomplish creation in one day. Genesis demonstrates an almighty God who spoke in the affirmative and had vision and order for what He desired to manifest. Therefore, as you start to think about creating your own world, you must be sure of what you want.

Be careful not to waiver or even entertain doubt. You must speak and move in the affirmative. Although you may want to address every area of your life at one time, it is important that you have order and are therefore focused on specific areas at a set time. In the next chapter, you will learn exactly how you can use the divine strategies from Genesis to create your world just like God the Creator did.

Follow God's Divine Strategy in Genesis 1

HOW TO CREATE YOUR OWN WORLD

Before you begin this process, there are two important factors that you must do. First, as discussed at the beginning of this book, **you must believe so that you speak in faith.** The second thing that **you must do is forgive yourself and others**. In order to create as your heavenly Father did, you always should operate from a place of love, which includes having a clean heart.

"And when you stand praying, if you hold anything against anyone, forgive them, so that your Father in heaven may forgive you your sins" Mark 11:25.

Now that you believe and forgave, the book of Genesis gives you divine instructions— a blueprint to creating the world you desire. If you read the first chapter of this book, you will see that when God created the world, He stood in His power and authority, using His words, vision, and order. You can use God's example to design the life you desire.

Like creation, each day of the week Monday through Saturday, you will be creating through words and vision. Each day should be designated for a particular area of your life. Remember, you have 6 days, and 24 hours in each day. You do not have to cram everything into one day! All day, you will focus your words, (positive and affirmative) prayers, scripture, and visualization on those specific areas for that day. Although your life may be presently out of order, use your words every day to call it to order.

Example:

Monday: Health (Mental, Physical, Emotional)

Tuesday: Marriage and Home

Wednesday: Children or Family

Thursday: Finances

Friday: Business

Saturday: Needs of Others (Prayer Requests)

Sunday: Rest and Praise—Give Thanks!

For each day, it is important that you speak God's word (scriptures) as it pertains to that area. Find the scripture that pertains to your situation. For example: if Monday is the day you designated to speak about your overall health, you can use the scripture Isaiah 53:5, "But He was wounded for [my] transgressions, He was bruised for [my] iniquities; the chastisement of [my] peace was upon Him and with His stripes [I] am healed." Finally, on the last day, Sunday, you will rest and give God thanks for a good week.

"And God saw all that He had made, and it was very good" Genesis 1:31.

"Let's begin creating your world. Refer to the example given on page 44 for inspiration. Write the focus area for each day and the scripture that you will use to support your daily declaration"

Day 1: Monday

Day 2: Tuesday

Day 3: Wednesday

Day 4: Thursday

Day 5: Friday

Day 6: Saturday

Day 7: Sunday
Rest and Praise—give thanks!

This life-changing book was not designed for a week, a month, or even a year of instruction, but for a lifetime. Now that you've read and completed the steps given for divine strategies as to how to create the world you desire, get ready to read real-life testimonies from real people.

These people have tried the strategies given in this book and have seen the manifestation of the victory needed in their lives—from children to adults.

TESTIMONIES

A TESTIMONY OF A READER

God is so thoughtful toward us! Pastor Kinloch asked me to read this book at a time that I was embarking on a major transition in my career and a move toward becoming an entrepreneur. As I read, I felt like God was revealing the strategy needed to take me through this new phase of life. In preparation for the journey, I have sought the Lord for specific things, but not as specific as indicated in this book. Thank you to Pastor Kinloch for laboring for this revelation and allowing God to use her to deliver it, not only to God's Way, but to the world.

This book reminds us that absolutely nothing presented to us in scripture is just casual or random. Every word, action, theme, and context has meaning. Seeking out the meaning is like finding treasure. Meditating on the revelations shared in this book is like finding treasure. And it is the exact treasure that we need for a time such as this. Every day, both in our personal lives and in the world, we see the results of the work of the enemy and the fallen nature of man. If you stare too intently at these circumstances, you will certainly swoon. This book teaches us to not accept this reality, but to partner with a reality that is consistent with living in the Kingdom of God. We learn to walk in the authority that we were given and to not give up, no matter what we see or feel. Finally, we also learn to face ourselves, not in fear of what we will see, but with hope that the God who created the universe is able to resurrect, renew and refresh us as we confess and stand on His word. I am challenged to stop sabotaging myself and to forgive myself and anyone that I have been holding an ought against. It's time to move forward with purpose and intentionality.

—K.S.

I AM AN HONOR ROLL STUDENT

I attend Miracle Academy School. When I was in school, my math grade was very bad. The math was easy at first and then it got very hard, and I got a D. I prayed every night and asked God to help me. In the morning, I said my confessions before I went to school. My mom told me to always pray and watch what I say. After doing this, the bad grades went away, and I got a B!

It was the highest grade I have ever gotten in my whole entire life in math. I was the top student in math, and I'm going to 5th grade, and I know next year I will get all good grades in math because I watch what I say, and I will always watch what I say and not say bad things about myself and other people. I'll always be nice and always encourage people to watch what they say and not say bad things. I got the wristband from our pastor, and I wear it every day to help me remember.

No more bad grades for me in 5th grade. I will be on the honor roll!

-J. Gambrell

FINANCIAL BLESSING

A couple of weeks ago, Pastor Kinloch gave us wristbands to wear. She explained to us that for the next 21 days we were to "Watch what we say" and choose a consistent time to pray for our needs. She told us that God wanted us to be specific in our prayers. We were instructed to use each day, Monday through Saturday, to focus on certain areas of our lives, and on Sundays, we would give God praise for answering our prayers. We followed these instructions for three weeks.

Every Wednesday, I chose to specifically pray about my finances. I remember saying to God each Wednesday, "I need a financial miracle" and I said, "I need you to just blow my mind financially." I reminded God that I continually pay my tithes and give my offering and that I have planted seeds in the ground. I said, "You promised me a prophet's reward." I genuinely believed that God heard my prayers.

Then I had a special dream on the Friday leading up to our Sunday day of praise for answered prayers. In this dream, I took a friend and her daughter to visit relatives that were out of town. When we got to the place where the relatives lived, a lady at the house was so happy that I took the time to bring my friend and her daughter to visit that she wanted to pay me for bringing them.

I told her that she did not have to pay me because I didn't mind bringing them. She said, "No, I'm going to give you some silver coins." Again, I told her that she did not have to do that. She reached into her pocket and pulled out a stack of silver coins and again I refused to accept the silver coins. She said that she wanted to do this and shoved the coins in my hand. As the visit was winding up, I embraced the woman, and she thanked me for bringing my friend and her daughter for the visit again. As I embraced the woman, I slipped the coins back into her pocket and she said, "Why did you do that?" Then she said, "That is okay. I know what I am going to do. Let me get my checkbook and sow a seed to you." That is the only way that I would take money from her. But before I could see the amount of the check, I woke up out of the dream.

We don't share every dream that we have, but sometimes God will lead us to share a particular dream so that when it comes to pass, we will have a witness that we had the dream or the vision. So, on Sunday, at the end of the 21 days, I thanked God because the wristband was just a symbol of what God can do for us. God is so true to His word. I received that financial blessing in real life, and it blew my mind. That is what I asked Him to do. God did it and it was super abundantly above all that I could ask. I believed God, and He has shown Himself to be faithful. This is just the beginning, as it is the season for the people of God!

-C. Lawyer

POSITIVE INFLUENCE

The Lord instructed Pastor Kinloch to give us wristbands to wear for 21 days as a reminder to "Watch what you say." One of my students, who is in the second grade, asked me, "why do you wear that band all the time?" I said to her, "it reminds me to watch what I am saying because my words matter, and God wants me to say the right words." She said to me, "I want one of those because I want to watch what I say and say good things and not bad things." Yes, kids do pay attention to what we say and do and how we carry ourselves as a witness of Jesus Christ. Therefore, the wristbands are also an evangelistic tool for witnessing and spreading the good news.

-D. Mitchell

BLESSED BUSINESS OWNER

A few weeks ago, God gave Pastor Kinloch a series, on watching what you say. The congregation received instructions to go home and write out and say what we wanted God to do, speak positive things only, and every Sunday it would be praise day! We were given a bracelet that would serve as a reminder to watch what we say. I followed the instructions.

I designated Tuesday as the day to speak over my catering business. In the second week of speaking over my business, I received a call from the manager of a major business franchise location with a special request. The manager indicated that it was short notice but wanted to know if it was possible for me to provide one hundred cupcakes for his establishment!

I accepted the job. As I started to bake, God gave me step-by-step instructions as to what to do.

I did it as God had instructed and the outcome was amazing! The manager and his staff were well pleased. Within the same week, I got a call for another catering job, and by the end of the week, I got a call from another caterer that was overbooked and gave me the job she could not take.

My heart is overflowing with joy and the awesomeness of our Heavenly Father. I am grateful to be under a leader that is obedient to God! Each day I am speaking over my life and this small bracelet has certainly helped to bring BIG changes. This practice has allowed me to cancel all the negative speaking and to only speak positivity over my life! I believe and speak that I will be blessed to be a blessing to others and to the Kingdom of God! Thank you, God, for enlarging my borders!

-K. Richardson

HIS FAITHFULNESS TOWARDS ME!

I am beyond grateful for the sermon that came forth entitled, "Watch What You Say!" I knew it would change my world! That evening, the Lord laid upon my heart to sow a special seed. I followed His lead and meditated on the Word. That night, I outlined my week on which areas of my life I would be speaking to each day.

I went to Genesis 1 to read the account of creation as God spoke the world into existence. Surely, if the Holy Spirit instructed us to speak each day what we wanted, it would be so. With much excitement and strong belief, each day I spoke and spoke. The bracelet was a constant reminder to keep speaking.

One Friday, before getting out of bed, I spoke to our Father about my needs, and I told Him I was going to trust Him that day for it. It did not matter what I saw, I spoke what I wanted. Within hours, I received that which I had declared by faith. It came to me! I marvel at our God and His faithfulness toward me.

This series greatly blessed me and stirred my faith. It affirms that if we do believe the word of God, and believe His prophet, we will prosper.

-S. Carson

71

TRANSFORMATION HAPPENING IN MY FAMILY

This is my testimony of how good God has been to my family and I. Pastor Kinloch gave us wristbands four weeks ago to remind us to "Watch What We Say." She prayed over them as a reminder to trust God and to be specific in what we wanted God to do for us. I let my family know about the wristbands and how to put their requests before God and to watch what they say.

On Sunday, we collectively put our wristbands on at a certain time depending on where we lived. Some family members put on their bracelets at 3 pm, others at 2 pm, and noon for the West Coast. We prayed for 21 days with each day lifting up a specific request. On Sunday we thanked God. Personally, I have been praying for my family and believing that they will know God more, for good health, prosperity and for the businesses in the family. This was an opportunity for all of us to be on one accord.

I sent this message to them and told them that we must be on one accord. As a result of this, I have seen growth. I have also witnessed the start of a new business for one family member and spiritual growth for others. We are moving forward to do the things that we desire as a family because we were praying for each other and believing that God was able to do it.

-L.C.

HOW TO REQUEST YOUR FREE WRISTBAND

To request your free wristband, visit us on the web at www.godswaywoc.org or write us at;

1552 Boston Grill Road,

Mount Pleasant, South Carolina, 29466

IN LOVING MEMORY

In memory of two special persons who played a significant role in my life: my sister, Teretha Rosa Richardson and niece, Melissha I. Richardson